12|11

Mathemagic!

NUMBER TRICKS

Written by Lynda Colgan

Illustrated by Jane Kurisu

Kids Can Press

**With appreciation to the many teachers along the way
who made mathematics magical and fun — L.C.**

Text © 2011 Lynda Colgan
Illustrations © 2011 Jane Kurisu

Kids Can Press acknowledges the financial support of the Government of Ontario, through the Ontario Media Development Corporation's Ontario Book Initiative; the Ontario Arts Council; the Canada Council for the Arts; and the Government of Canada, through the BPIDP, for our publishing activity.

Published in Canada by
Kids Can Press Ltd.
25 Dockside Drive
Toronto, ON M5A 0B5

Published in the U.S. by
Kids Can Press Ltd.
2250 Military Road
Tonawanda, NY 14150

www.kidscanpress.com

Edited by Karen Li and Samantha Swenson
Designed by Julia Naimska

This book is smyth sewn casebound.
Manufactured in Altona, Manitoba, Canada, in 10/2011 by Friesens Corporation

CM 11 0 9 8 7 6 5 4 3

Library and Archives Canada Cataloguing in Publication

Colgan, Lynda, 1953–
Mathemagic! : number tricks / Lynda Colgan ;
illustrated by Jane Kurisu.

ISBN 978-1-55453-425-8

1. Mathematical recreations—Juvenile literature. I. Kurisu, Jane II. Title.

QA95.C598 2011   j793.74   C2010-904986-1

Kids Can Press is a *Corus*™ Entertainment company

Contents

Introduction

If you're like most people, you probably think that doing math with your fingers is for babies and that "sticks and stones" have no use beyond "breaking bones."

If you're like most people, you've probably been outsmarted by one of those "human calculator" know-it-alls. You know the type: the brainiac who can compute answers in her head before you can even say "multiplication."

If you're like most people, you've probably never used a bone to multiply, and you've probably never used X-ray vision to see through dice. Because if you're like most people, you didn't know you could — until now.

Here's the great news: YOU don't have to be like most people! By learning the secrets in this book, YOU will be computing answers at breakneck speed, plucking secret numbers from your friends' minds and using the mysterious mathematical secrets of the ancient Egyptians.

All you'll need are a handful of beans, a finger or two and some well-practiced steps. Then *Mathakazam!* You'll become the rarest kind of conjurer: not one of those run-of-the-mill, bunny-in-a-hat, vanishing-scarf types, but a true-blue mathemagician. What are you waiting for? Let's get started!

Digital Wizardry

Have you ever noticed how a good magician's hands are always moving? Sleight of hand is the cornerstone of good magic. So before the big show, warm up your digits with these quick multiplying tricks.

Multiplying by 9

1 Hold up your hands with palms facing you. Number the fingers from left to right as 1 to 10.

2 Hold down the finger of the number you want to multiply by 9. In this example, we want to multiply 9 x 7, so we drop finger 7.

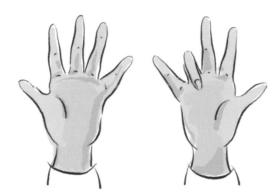

The fingers to the left of the dropped digit are the tens, and the fingers to the right are the ones, or units. In this example, there are 6 fingers to the left and 3 to the right. So 9 x 7 = 63.

Want another example? Here is how you would multiply 9 x 3 using your fingers. Drop finger number 3. There are 2 fingers to the left and 7 to the right. 9 x 3 = 27.

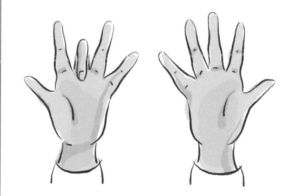

Try this trick with the other numbers in the 9 times table!

Multiplying by 6 'n' up

1 Hold your hands with palms up and fingers toward one another. Number the fingers on each hand from bottom to top as 6 to 9.

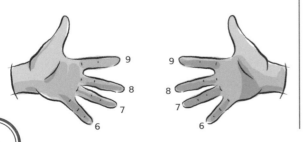

2 Now touch the two fingers that represent the numbers that you want to multiply. In this example, we want to multiply 8 x 8. So finger number 8 on one hand touches finger number 8 on the other hand.

3 To do the calculation, first add the fingers below, including the ones that touch. Here, there are 6 of them: 3 on one hand and 3 on the other. These are the tens. 6 x 10 = 60.

4 Now look at the fingers above the ones that touch, including the thumbs. Multiply the number of fingers on the left hand (in this case, 2) by the number of fingers on the right hand (also 2). These are the units. 2 x 2 = 4.

Add this to the 60 you've already got, and that makes 64.

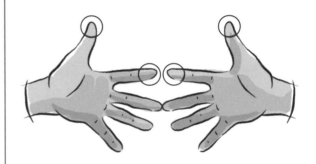

How do these tricks work?

Part of the secret to the first trick is that when we multiply a number by 9, the first digit in the product is always 1 less than that number.

For example,

8 x 9 = 72, and 8 − 1 = 7

3 x 9 = 27, and 3 − 1 = 2

The other part of the secret lies in a quirk about multiples of 9: the sum of their digits always equals 9.

For example, take the number 18:

1 + 8 = 9

How about the number 36?

3 + 6 = 9

When we hold down a finger to multiply by 9, we are basically subtracting 1 from the number being multiplied. So the fingers to the left of the dropped finger give the first number of your product. Then the number it takes to add up to 9 is your second number — that's the number of fingers to the right of the dropped digit.

In the second trick, we are using a system called complementary arithmetic. It was described by the artist and inventor Leonardo da Vinci in the 1500s and was used throughout medieval Europe.

If you are multiplying 8 x 6, you would hold your hands this way.

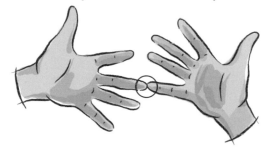

Leonardo would have charted the same equation like this:

First, write the two numbers you want to multiply. These are called factors (the math name for numbers that multiply with other numbers to make a third number).

Then subtract each factor from 10. The difference is called the ten-complement.

Factor	Ten-complement
8	**2**
6	**4**

Next, subtract the ten-complement of one factor from the other factor. In this case, either 8 − 4 or 6 − 2. The result is 4, the digit for the "Tens" column. Finally, multiply the ten-complements (in this case, 2 x 4). This gives 8, the value in the "Units" column.

Tens	Units
8	2
6	4
4	*8*

The answer? 8 x 6 = 48. When you use your fingers, you are acting out this method.

Mind Games

Now that you've warmed up, let's get started with some (almost) foolproof tricks that will convince people that you can read their minds! Your audience may need paper and pencils to keep track of their calculations.

Two true

In this trick, your audience members start with their own secret numbers. But everyone ends up with the same final number!

1 Ask each member of the audience to think of a secret number.

2 Tell them to add 4 to the secret number, then multiply the sum by 4.

3 Now ask your audience to subtract 8 and then divide the difference by 4.

4 Give them some time to work out their new number. Finally, have the audience subtract their original secret number from their new number.

5 Tell them to concentrate on this final number. Tell them to picture it so that you can see it clearly in their minds. Then you can tell them, "*Mathakazam!* You are thinking of the number 2!"

Enjoy their gasps of disbelief before you move on to your next trick.

Seeing elephants

1 Ask each member of your audience to think of a secret number and keep it private. Any number will do, but a small one may be easiest to work with.

Now, ask them to double their number. Next have them add 8 and then divide the new number by 2. Instruct your audience to subtract their original secret number from the number they have now.

2 Tell your audience to find the letter in the alphabet that corresponds to this new number. That is, if their new number is 1, they should think of the letter A. If their new number is 2, they should think of the letter B. 3 = C, 4 = D, 5 = E and so on.

Ask them to think of a country name that starts with their letter.

3 Now ask your audience to identify the second letter in the country name and have them imagine an animal that lives in that country. Finally, ask them to think of the color of that animal.

4 Now it's time to read their minds! Announce, *"Mathakazam!* You should all be thinking of the same animal ... But I think something went wrong. Because what I'm seeing doesn't make sense: there are no gray elephants in Denmark!"

SECRET TO SUCCESS

Move your audience quickly through this mind game. This leaves them with little time to think about a country or an animal. In fact, there aren't many countries that begin with D, which is why Denmark is chosen most often. (The others are Dominica, Dominican Republic, Democratic Republic of Congo and Djibouti.) The same goes for animals starting with E. (Some others are emu, eel and eagle.)

How does this trick work?

These tricks can be easily explained with diagrams. We'll use ◆ to represent the secret numbers. Take a look at how the first trick breaks down.

Step 1: Think of a secret number.

◆

Step 2: Add 4.

◆ + ●●●●

Step 3: Multiply by 4. (Think 4 times the diagram.)

◆ ●●●●
◆ ●●●●
◆ ●●●●
◆ ●●●●

Step 4: Subtract 8.

◆ ●●
◆ ●●
◆ ●●
◆ ●●

Step 5: Divide by 4.

◆ ●●

Step 6: Subtract your secret number.

●●

Step 7: What number do you have?

2

Working with a symbol to represent the secret number in the trick allows us to focus on the steps in the instructions instead of focusing on calculations. This symbol is called a variable in math. It is often written as x or y, and it stands for possible numbers that could satisfy a problem.

Diagramming is a good strategy for making up your own secret-number tricks. Start with a few small tiles, bread tags or bottle caps to represent your secret number and its multiples. Then use a handful of beads or beans to act out the calculations.

MIND-BOGGLING FEATS WITH EVERYDAY FACTS

Use phone numbers and birthdays as secret numbers to give your tricks a personal touch. For example, say, "Think of a secret number between 1 and 100. Now take your age, multiply it by 2, add 5, multiply by 50 and subtract 365. Next, add your original secret number, and then add 115 to the total. *Mathakazam!* The first half of the final number is your age, and the other part is your secret number!"

Now let's diagram the second trick.

Step 1: Think of a secret number.

Step 2: Double the secret number.

Step 3: Add 8.

Step 4: Divide by 2. (Think of one-half of the diagram.)

Step 5: Subtract the original secret number.

●●●●

No matter what number a person starts with, he will always end up with 4 as the final answer if he follows the instructions correctly. The number 4 brings him to the letter D and — most likely — to the bizarre idea of a gray elephant in Denmark!

CLOSE CALLS

This second trick is not 100% foolproof. Sometimes other answers will arise (like a brown owl in Dominica), and sometimes mistakes are made (so a person thinks of a silver armadillo in Canada), but you can usually cover for the few oddball responses by claiming that the majority's answer sounds by far the loudest to a mind-reading mathemagician.

Calculator Magic

For these next tricks, your audience will get to use calculators. But there will be no technological aids for you. Instead, outwit everyone with your superior computational skills!

The secret of 73

1 Secretly write the number 73 on a piece of paper. Fold it up and give it to an audience member to keep safe.

2 Ask for a volunteer assistant. Hand her a calculator. Turn away so that you cannot see the numbers she is punching into the calculator.

3 Tell your assistant to pick any 4-digit number and enter it twice into the calculator. For example, 12341234.

4 Close your eyes, rub your temples and announce, "The number on the screen is divisible by 137!" Ask your assistant to verify your claim by dividing the number by 137 and then shouting "Yes" or "No." (The answer will be "Yes.")

5 Now ask your assistant if she can divide this new number by her original 4-digit number, which in this case means entering 1234. "Yes or no?" (The answer will be "Yes.")

6 Finally, say, *"Mathakazam!"* and ask the first audience member to read aloud the number you wrote on paper. Then ask your assistant, "Does my prediction match the number on the calculator display?" The answer will be "Yes!"

Fortune-telling

1 Find someone in the audience who would like her fortune told. Hand your volunteer a calculator. Then stand far away from her and have other members of the audience blindfold you.

2 Ask your volunteer to secretly select a 3-digit number and then enter it twice into the calculator. For example, 123123.

3 Next tell your volunteer that she must carefully follow your instructions to divine her future. Rub your temples, and then ask if the number on the calculator display is divisible by 11. Your volunteer should enter ÷ 11 on the calculator. If she is not sure how to answer, ask her if the number on the display is a whole number. If it is, her answer should be "Yes."

4 Rub your temples again, and then ask if the new number on the calculator display is divisible by 13. (The answer will be "Yes.")

5 For the grand finale, ask your volunteer to divide this final number by the original 3-digit number. Then call out, "*Mathakazam!* The final answer is … lucky number 7!"

If you wish to predict bad luck for your volunteer, have her divide by 7 instead of 13 in step 4. Her final answer will be unlucky number 13.

SECRET TO SUCCESS

For the best effect on your audience, wear a blindfold or stand behind a screen that separates you from your volunteer. Keep your hands in the air so the audience can see that you're not using a hidden calculator.

How do these tricks work?

The secret of 73 works because entering any 4-digit number twice is the same thing as multiplying it by 10001. For example, we used 1234 as our secret number.

$$1234 \times 10001 = 12341234$$

Now you know that the volunteer's 8-digit number is divisible by the original 4-digit number and by 10001. And 10001 can be further divided into 137 and 73. This division can be expressed more clearly in a factor tree:

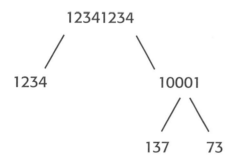

Any volunteer's 8-digit number will always be divisible by the original 4-digit number, 137 and secret number 73.

Our fortune-telling trick works in much the same way. Entering a 3-digit number twice is equivalent to multiplying it by 1001. In our example, we used 123.

$$123 \times 1001 = 123123$$

What are the factors of 1001?

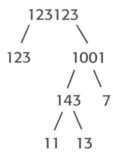

Since $1001 = 11 \times 13 \times 7$, the 6-digit number will be divisible by the original 3-digit number, 11, 13 … and lucky number 7!

For these tricks, we used trees to find the prime factors of 10001 (137 and 73) and the prime factors of 1001 (7, 11 and 13).

PRIME-FACTOR FINDING

If a counting number has only two different factors, 1 and itself, then the number is said to be prime. Those numbers that have more than two different factors (e.g., 10, which has factors 1, 10, 2 and 5) are called composite numbers. Every composite number can be expressed as the product of prime numbers. No matter how you choose to factor a number (i.e., to find all of its divisors), the results will be the same. Look at these two factor trees for 60:

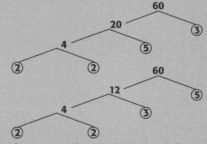

When you have finished factoring 60, you will always have the same prime factors at the tips of the tree: 2, 2, 3 and 5.

SIEVE OF ERATOSTHENES

If you're not sure whether a counting number is prime or composite, there is a sure way to check: use a sieve — and not the kind that you use in the kitchen to drain water from pasta! This special sieve drains out the composite numbers, leaving only the prime numbers. It was invented by an ancient Greek mathematician, astronomer and librarian, Eratosthenes (276–194 BCE), whose other claim to fame was being the first person to accurately estimate the diameter of Earth.

Start by copying this chart of the counting numbers from 1 to 100:

1	2	3	4	5	6	7	8	9	10
11	12	13	14	15	16	17	18	19	20
21	22	23	24	25	26	27	28	29	30
31	32	33	34	35	36	37	38	39	40
41	42	43	44	45	46	47	48	49	50
51	52	53	54	55	56	57	58	59	60
61	62	63	64	65	66	67	68	69	70
71	72	73	74	75	76	77	78	79	80
81	82	83	84	85	86	87	88	89	90
91	92	93	94	95	96	97	98	99	100

1 Cross out 1 because it is a special case, neither prime nor composite.

2 Circle 2 because it is a prime. Then cross out all the multiples of 2 (i.e., 4, 6, 8, 10, 12 and so on) — in other words, every second number.

3 Circle 3 because it is a prime. Then cross out all the multiples of 3 (every third number). You will find that some numbers, such as, 6, 12 and 18, will already be crossed out because they are also multiples of 2.

4 Circle the next open number: 5, a prime. Then cross out all the multiples of 5 (every fifth number).

5 Continue these steps until all the numbers between 1 and 100 have either been circled or crossed out.

When you are finished, you will have circled all the prime numbers between 1 and 100. You can also use a sieve to find all the prime numbers between 101 and 200, and 201 and 300, and so on.

Roll 'em!

Round up as many dice as you can for this trick. You'll also need a hat, a piece of paper, an envelope, a pencil and two volunteer assistants.

1 Ask one assistant to collect the dice and place them in a hat. Have him shake the hat to mix up the dice, then select any 2 dice and place them carefully on the table.

2 Turn your back to the table to show your audience you aren't watching. Then ask your second assistant to roll the 2 dice and then stack them vertically.

3 Turn around as if to check that your assistants have followed your instructions: Do you see one die placed on top of the other? As you do this, make a mental note of the number of dots on the top face in the stack.

4 Again, turn away from the table. Pull the piece of paper from your pocket and show that there is nothing written on it. Tell your audience that you are about to ask your assistant a question, but that you'll already have predicted the answer.

5 Write down your answer, fold the paper into quarters, slip it into an envelope and hand the envelope to an audience member for safekeeping.

6 Still facing away from the table, call out to your dice-rolling assistant. Ask him to look at the 2-dice tower. Does he agree that there are 3 faces of the dice that no one can see — the 1 against the tabletop and the 2 that are touching?

7 Next, ask your assistant to find the sum of the 3 hidden faces and then to tell you and the audience that number.

8 Finally, turn to the audience member who is holding the envelope. Ask her to read your prediction out loud. *Mathakazam!* Of course that number will be the sum of the 3 hidden faces!

SECRET TO SUCCESS

Before you begin this trick, let your audience members roll the dice as many times as they'd like. It's essential that everyone has a chance to see that you are not using trick dice. Who needs phony dice when you have mathemagic?

How does this trick work?

Unlike most people, you — the keeper of many ancient and little-known mathematical secrets — know that the opposite faces on a die always add up to 7.

In other words, 1 is always directly opposite 6, 5 is opposite 2, and 3 is opposite 4. By looking at one face, you know what is on the opposite side, since the sum of opposite faces is always 7.

This means that if you add 2 opposite faces of 2 dice, the total will be 14, or 2 x 7.

Since you glanced at the stack of dice and made a mental note of the value of the top face, you can quickly calculate the sum of the 3 hidden faces by subtracting that number from 14.

For example, if the top face on your stack of dice shows 5 dots, all you have to do is subtract 5 from 14 to get the sum of the 3 hidden faces.

14 - 5 = 9

DIVINING WITH THE TALUS BONE

Did you know that playing with dice is sometimes called rolling the bones? This expression (as well as the word *talisman*) comes from the fact that the earliest dice were 4-sided sheep anklebones called talus bones. In ancient Greece and Rome, people would toss the bone and bet on which side it would land.

Archaeologists have discovered ancient versions of the 6-sided dice we use today made of bone, horn, ivory, stone, wood and amber in excavations all around the world (including in Egypt, England, India, China and Greece) dating back to 3000 BCE.

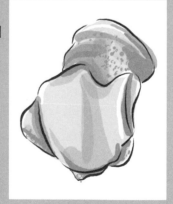

If you want to convince the audience that you are a genuine genius, ask for a new volunteer. This time, ask the volunteer to roll 3 dice and stack them into a tower. Again, turn your back to show that you aren't looking.

Once your assistant is ready, pretend to check if she's followed your instructions. At the same time, make note of the number of dots on the top face.

Follow the same steps as before: write your number on scrap paper and hand it to a member of the audience. Then ask your assistant to find the sum of the 5 hidden faces: the 1 facing the tabletop and the 4 that are touching.

You know that the opposite faces of a die add up to 7. Therefore, the total sum of the opposite faces of 3 dice will be 21, or 3 x 7. Subtract the number of dots on the top face of the top die from 21. This gives you the sum of the 5 hidden faces.

ADD-ITIONAL DICE DEVIOUSNESS

If you dare, you can repeat this trick with 4, 5, 6 or 7 dice, since you know the total sum of the opposite sides of 1 or more die is always a multiple of 7. All you need to do is quickly glance at the top number and subtract it from the correct multiple.

Your part in the trick is easy — it's your volunteer who needs a steady hand. You don't want that tower of dice tumbling down before your prediction is ready!

Magic Number 9

Nine is a very interesting number. It is *special* because it is the largest single-digit number in our counting system, but it is *magical* (as you will see) because it has properties that none of the digits from 0 to 8 have. In this trick, we use the unusual properties of the number 9 and reveal your prediction without saying a word.

1 To prepare for this trick, write *"Mathakazam!"* on a sticky note and adhere it to page 9 of any paperback novel. Prepare a paperback novel for each member of the audience, and then slip the books underneath the audience's seats before the show.

2 Once it comes time to perform the trick, ask your audience members to each think of a 4-digit number in which each digit is different. Tell them to write down their numbers and keep them secret. (We'll use 3741 as an example.)

3 Ask audience members to jumble up the 4 digits. If the new number is larger than the original number, have them write it above the original number. If the new number is smaller than the original number, have them write it below.

3741
1743

4 Now tell them to subtract the smaller number from the larger number.

$$3741 - 1743 \over 1998$$

5 Instruct them to take the difference and add the digits together.

$$1 + 9 + 9 + 8 = 27$$

If their total is a 2-digit number, then they must add these 2 digits together as well. Keep them adding until they are left with a single-digit number.

$$2 + 7 = 9$$

6 For the finale, say to the audience, "Concentrate on this number. This is your new secret number. *Think only of this single-digit number.*" Tell your audience to look under their seats, pick up their books and open them to the same page as their secret number.

They will open their books to page 9 and see a note from you that reads, *"Mathakazam!"*

SECRET TO SUCCESS

Tricks like this are most impressive when everyone has a chance to be surprised. One way to make sure that no one peeks or whispers to a neighbor and spoils the shocker is to arrange the chairs in a circle, alternating them so that one chair faces toward the center of the circle and the next faces out.

How does this trick work?

The secret behind this trick is the Nine Principle. Reverse the digits of any 2-digit number. Then subtract the smaller number from the larger one. The difference will always be a multiple of 9. Take a look at the following examples:

$$43 - 34 = 9 \text{ (which is } 9 \times 1\text{)}$$
$$86 - 68 = 18 \text{ (which is } 9 \times 2\text{)}$$

Move around the digits of a 3-digit number, and then subtract the smaller number from the larger one. The difference will still be a multiple of 9. Take a look:

$$321 - 213 = 108 \text{ (which is } 9 \times 12\text{)}$$
$$321 - 123 = 198 \text{ (which is } 9 \times 22\text{)}$$

The Nine Principle works with 4-digit numbers, too:

$$4321 - 1234 = 3087 \text{ (which is } 9 \times 343\text{)}$$
$$4321 - 2431 = 1890 \text{ (which is } 9 \times 210\text{)}$$

Note that in each case, the sum of the digits in the difference is also 9. For example,

$$86 - 68 = 18 \text{ and } 1 + 8 = 9$$
$$321 - 123 = 198, \text{ and } 1 + 9 + 8 = 18.$$
Then add the digits of 18: $1 + 8 = 9$.

No matter how your audience mixes up their digits, they will always end up with the magic number 9.

SECRET TO SUCCESS

If you want to heighten audience suspense, go online to find a sound file of a drumroll. Play it every time you are about to announce an answer. As soon as the cymbals crash, call out, *"Mathakazam!* The magic number is ..."

Here's a variation on this trick to keep your audience amazed!

1 Have a member of the audience pick a 4-digit number. Ask her to mix up the digits to form a new number, and then tell her to subtract the smaller number from the larger one.

2 Ask her to tell you all the digits of the difference in any order, omitting a digit — any digit she wants, as long as it's not 0.

For example, if she picked 6759 as her secret number and 5796 as her mixed-up version of that number, then 6759 − 5796 = 963.

If she said that 6 and 9 were 2 digits in the difference, then you could instantly tell the audience that 3 is the missing number.

How?

You know from the Nine Principle that the sum of the digits in the difference should equal 9. Since 6 + 9 = 15, and the sum of those digits is 1 + 5 = 6, then you know the missing digit must be 3 (the difference of 9 − 6).

SECRET TO SUCCESS

There are many fun ways to choose an assistant. If you want to pick a helper randomly, face away from the audience and toss a table-tennis ball over your shoulder. Ask the person who catches the ball to join you on the stage.

Mummy Math

For this trick, you will need a large sheet of paper, a marker and an assistant who is able to double numbers. Offer a calculator if the numbers get too big — after all, not everyone has your amazing powers!

1 Ask the audience for a 2-digit by 2-digit multiplication question. For this example, we'll use 34 x 14.

2 Divide your paper into two columns. Write the numbers 1 and 34 in the first row. Then ask your volunteer to double those numbers in the next row. The paper will look like this:

| 1 | 34 |
| 2 | 68 |

Doubling each row will give you this:

1	34
2	68
4	136
8	272

3 Encourage the audience to help your assistant by shouting out the doubled numbers. But you can stop listening when the number in the left column produces a number that is bigger than the multiplier in the 2-digit multiplication question.

Here, we stopped listening at 8 because the next doubling would produce 16, which is bigger than our multiplier, 14.

4 Now find the numbers in the left column that add to 14. Here, you have 8 + 4 + 2. Then look across to the right column and add the corresponding numbers: 272 + 136 + 68. Keep your answer private.

5 Quiet the room and announce that you have the product: 34 x 14 = 476. Your audience will be baffled because the chart doesn't give away your secret method.

SECRET TO SUCCESS

For this trick, you'll need to brush up on your human calculator skills. To add numbers such as 272 + 136 + 68 in your head, use this simple strategy: work from left to right, adding the digits in the hundreds, tens and units columns separately as you go. Be sure to keep a running total.

Start with the hundreds:
200 + 100 = 300.
(Running total: 300)

Add the tens: 70 + 30 + 60 = 160.
(Running total: 300 + 160 = 460)

Add the units: 2 + 6 + 8 = 16.
(Grand total: 460 + 16 = 476)

How does this trick work?

This magical method of multiplying two numbers is more than old: it's ancient. It was invented by the ancient Egyptians. This method is still used in many rural communities in Ethiopia, Russia, the Arab world and the Near East.

The early Egyptians used addition to get the answer to a multiplication problem. The trick works by using a secret about doubling numbers.

Let's use ◆ to represent the number you want to multiply. Take a look at the chart on the right to see what happens when you double.

◆	1◆
◆ ◆	2◆ (which means 2 x ◆)
◆ ◆ ◆ ◆	4◆ (which means 4 x ◆)
◆ ◆ ◆ ◆ ◆ ◆ ◆ ◆	8◆ (which means 8 x ◆)
◆ ◆ ◆ ◆ ◆ ◆ ◆ ◆ ◆ ◆ ◆ ◆ ◆ ◆ ◆ ◆	16◆ (which means 16 x ◆)
◆ ◆ ◆ ◆ ◆ ◆ ◆ ◆ ◆ ◆ ◆ ◆ ◆ ◆ ◆ ◆ ◆ ◆ ◆ ◆ ◆ ◆ ◆ ◆ ◆ ◆ ◆ ◆ ◆ ◆ ◆ ◆	32◆ (which means 32 x ◆)

MUMMY SHORTCUTS

The ancient Egyptians didn't actually multiply by two every time they needed to complete an equation. Instead, they referred to large tables on which doublings of two were already recorded.

Amazingly, you can express any number in terms of the doubled numbers that precede it. For example,

15 ◆ is the same as 1◆ + 2◆ + 4◆ + 8◆.

10 ◆ is the same as 2◆ + 8◆.

Let's look at the trick on page 24. Ancient Egyptian multiplication uses two columns: we use the first column to find the doubled numbers that make up the multiplier (the number that you are multiplying). Here, the multiplier is 14. It can be expressed as 2 + 4 + 8.

1	34
2	68
4	136
8	272

Remember, 2◆ + 4◆ + 8◆ = 14◆. So we then add the corresponding doublings of the multiplicand (the number by which you are multiplying) in the second column.

So this: 2◆ + 4◆ + 8◆ = 14◆

Becomes this:
(2 x 34) + (4 x 34) + (8 x 34) = (14 x 34)

Becomes this:
68 + 136 + 272 = 476

And now you've discovered that the product of 14 and 34 is 476.

MATHEMAGICAL INCANTATIONS

Magicians use words such as *abracadabra* and *hocus-pocus* to suggest that they are casting a spell by using a secret language. Like magic, mathematics has its own special words, such as *multiplier* and *multiplicand, factor* and *product*. (Check out the glossary at the back of this book for more.) Knowing these words helps you to understand the secrets of each trick so that you can make up more tricks of your own. Bewilder the crowd by using math words, such as add-*akazam* or sum-*sala-bim,* in your "spells."

It's in the Cards

Card tricks always seem to arouse people's interest and curiosity. This is a cunning math card trick that you can carry around in your pocket. That way, whenever a dull or quiet moment presents itself, you can dazzle anyone who happens to be around.

1 To prepare for this trick, you will need to make a set of 6 cards like the ones shown on the opposite page. You can photocopy this set or make your own cards by using graph paper. Just be sure to copy the numbers exactly as you see them!

2 When it's time to begin, choose a volunteer. Give her the 6 cards, and ask her to pick a secret number between 1 and 63.

3 Ask her to give back all the cards that have her number on it.

4 Figure out the volunteer's secret number by adding together all the first numbers on the cards she gave back to you. (The first number is the top left-hand number on each card.)

For example, if she gave back cards 1, 3 and 4, then *Mathakazam!* Her secret number is 13. The first numbers on these cards are 1, 4 and 8, which add up to 13.

If she gave back cards 2, 5 and 6, then *Mathakazam!* Her secret number is 50. The first numbers on these cards are 2, 16 and 32, which add up to 50.

SECRET TO SUCCESS

To make this trick even more impressive, memorize the first number of each card. Then your volunteer won't even have to hand back the cards for you to guess her number. Instead, just ask her which cards have her number on them, and you can do the math in your head.

★★1★★

1	3	5	7	9	11	13
15	17	19	21	23	25	27
29	31	33	35	37	39	41
43	45	47	49	51	53	55
57	59	61	63			

★★2★★

2	3	6	7	10	11	14
15	18	19	22	23	26	27
30	31	34	35	38	39	42
43	46	47	50	51	54	55
58	59	62	63			

★★3★★

4	5	6	7	12	13	14
15	20	21	22	23	28	29
30	31	36	37	38	39	44
45	46	47	52	53	54	55
60	61	62	63			

★★4★★

8	9	10	11	12	13	14
15	24	25	26	27	28	29
30	31	40	41	42	43	44
46	46	47	56	57	58	59
60	61	62	63			

★★5★★

16	17	18	19	20	21	22
23	24	25	26	27	28	29
30	31	48	49	50	51	52
53	54	55	58	57	58	59
60	61	62	63			

★★6★★

32	33	34	35	36	37	38
39	40	41	42	43	44	45
46	47	48	49	50	51	52
53	54	55	56	57	58	59
60	61	62	63			

How does this trick work?

This trick is based on the binary number system. The word *binary* begins with *bi*, meaning two. We see *bi* in words such as *bicycle* (2 wheels) or *binocular* (2 eyes). *Binary* refers to numbers made up of only 2 digits: ones and zeros.

You're likely more familiar with the decimal system, in which we have 10 digits (0 to 9) to use in each place-value position. From left to right, the place-value positions are

Ten thousands	Thousands	Hundreds	Tens	Units

The number 547, for example, can be expanded to 5 hundreds + 4 tens + 7 units. Each position in the place-value chart is 10 times bigger than the position to its right.

Ten thousands	Thousands	Hundreds	Tens	Units
0	0	5	4	7

Binary numbers are special because they are made up of just 2 digits: ones and zeros. And each position in the place-value chart is *2 times* bigger than the position to its right.

Sixteens	Eights	Fours	Twos	Units

Moving from right to left in a binary number, we have a choice of using only the digits 0 or 1. For example, 19 in binary is written 10011. Adding from right to left, only the place values 1 + 2 + 16 will sum 19.

Sixteens	Eights	Fours	Twos	Units
1	0	0	1	1

BINARY SYSTEMS

Binary systems have a long history. In West Africa, people sent "telegraphs" via a combination of high- and low-pitched drumbeats. Some Aboriginal peoples in Australia and New Guinea counted by twos. And Morse code was developed with two symbols — dots and dashes — the combinations of which represent the letters of the alphabet.

Today, the binary number system is most widely used in computers because mechanical and electronic switches recognize only two states of operation, such as on/off or closed/open. An on/off switch allows current to flow only when it is in the closed (on) position. In binary code, the characters 1 and 0 stand for

1 = on/closed circuit/true
0 = off/open circuit/false

A place-value position marked with a 1 tells you to add that place value to make the final number. Values that do not contribute to the sum are skipped and marked with a 0. Here, we skip "Fours" and "Eights."

Now notice that the number 19 appears only on cards 1, 2 and 5. That is, 19 appears on the cards with first numbers 1, 2 and 16. It does not appear on the cards with first numbers 4, 8 or 32.

1	3	5	7	9	11	13
15	17	19	21	23	25	27
29	31	33	35	37	39	41
43	45	47	49	51	53	55
57	59	61	63			

★★**2**★★

2	3	6	7	10	11	14
15	18	19	22	23	26	27
30	31	34	35	38	39	42
43	46	47	50	51	54	55
58	59	62	63			

In this trick, each of the 6 cards corresponds to a binary place-value position. The numbers on the first card are the ones that would have a 1 in the "Units" position when written in binary. The numbers on the second card are the ones that would have a 1 in the "Twos" position when written in binary. The numbers on the third card would have a 1 in the "Fours" position when written in binary, and so on for the other cards.

So when you add up the first numbers on the cards that contain the "secret" number, you're simply adding the place values of a binary number!

★★**5**★★

16	17	18	19	20	21	22
23	24	25	26	27	28	29
30	31	48	49	50	51	52
53	54	55	58	57	58	59
60	61	62	63			

BINARY NUMBERS

Take a look at this chart to see how the numbers 1 through 25 are written in binary. Can you predict how larger numbers are represented in binary?

1	=	1	= 1
10	=	2 + 0	= 2
11	=	2 + 1	= 3
100	=	4 + 0 + 0	= 4
101	=	4 + 0 + 1	= 5
110	=	4 + 2 + 0	= 6
111	=	4 + 2 + 1	= 7
1000	=	8 + 0 + 0 + 0	= 8
1001	=	8 + 0 + 0 + 1	= 9
1010	=	8 + 0 + 2 + 0	= 10
1011	=	8 + 0 + 2 + 1	= 11
1100	=	8 + 4 + 0 + 0	= 12
1101	=	8 + 4 + 0 + 1	= 13
1110	=	8 + 4 + 2 + 0	= 14
1111	=	8 + 4 + 2 + 1	= 15
10000	=	16 + 0 + 0 + 0 + 0	= 16
10001	=	16 + 0 + 0 + 0 + 1	= 17
10010	=	16 + 0 + 0 + 2 + 0	= 18
10011	=	16 + 0 + 0 + 2 + 1	= 19
10100	=	16 + 0 + 4 + 0 + 0	= 20
10101	=	16 + 0 + 4 + 0 + 1	= 21
10110	=	16 + 0 + 4 + 2 + 0	= 22
10111	=	16 + 0 + 4 + 2 + 1	= 23
11000	=	16 + 8 + 0 + 0 + 0	= 24
11001	=	16 + 8 + 0 + 0 + 1	= 25

Boney Math

Multiply any numbers, no matter how many digits, without a calculator or computer. Simply divine the answer by arranging a set of Napier's magical multiplying bones.

1 To start, make yourself a set of magic Napier's bones or photocopy the ones on page 34.

2 Choose a volunteer assistant, and give him a marker and a notepad. Tell him that you will be in a trance and that he must write each digit you call out, from right to left.

3 Warm up by asking your audience members to give you a single-digit by multi-digit multiplication question. Let's say they give you 4 x 897.

From your bone collection, select the Index bone and bones number 8, 9 and 7 and lay them out.

Index	8	9	7
1	0 / 8	0 / 9	0 / 7
2	1 / 6	1 / 8	1 / 4
3	2 / 4	2 / 7	2 / 1
4	3 / 2	3 / 6	2 / 8
5	4 / 0	4 / 5	3 / 5
6	4 / 8	5 / 4	4 / 2
7	5 / 6	6 / 3	4 / 9
8	6 / 4	7 / 2	5 / 6
9	7 / 2	8 / 1	6 / 3

4 Look for the single-digit number in the Index (in this case, 4).

Then, as if in a trance, read the numbers in that row from right to left, adding the digits that align diagonally.

4	3 / 2	3 / 6	2 / 8

Here, you would read: 8, 8 (which is 2 + 6), 5 (which is 3 + 2) and 3. Your assistant should have written 3588, which is the product of 4 x 897! *Mathakazam!*

Try the bones with some larger numbers. Let's say your audience calls for the answer to 64 x 759. Quickly arrange your bones like this:

Index	7	5	9
1	0 / 7	0 / 5	0 / 9
2	1 / 4	1 / 0	1 / 8
3	2 / 1	1 / 5	2 / 7
4	2 / 8	2 / 0	3 / 6
5	3 / 5	2 / 5	4 / 5
6	**4 / 2**	**3 / 0**	**5 / 4**
7	4 / 9	3 / 5	6 / 3
8	5 / 6	4 / 0	7 / 2
9	6 / 3	4 / 5	8 / 1

First, focus on row 6, and read from right to left to get 4554.

Then focus on row 4, and read from right to left to get 3036. (In the hundreds diagonal, where $2 + 8 = 10$, simply note 0 and carry the 1 over to the thousands diagonal.)

Index	7	5	9
1	0 / 7	0 / 5	0 / 9
2	1 / 4	1 / 0	1 / 8
3	2 / 1	1 / 5	2 / 7
4	**2 / 8**	**2 / 0**	**3 / 6**
5	3 / 5	2 / 5	4 / 5
6	4 / 2	3 / 0	5 / 4
7	4 / 9	3 / 5	6 / 3
8	5 / 6	4 / 0	7 / 2
9	6 / 3	4 / 5	8 / 1

Line up the two numbers this way (or show your assistant how to do so beforehand):

```
4  5  5  4
   3  0  3  6
```

Add the numbers together, and *Mathakazam!* The product is 48 576.

How does this trick work?

This multiplication trick is at least 400 years old. The original multiplying bones were invented by a Scottish mathematician named John Napier. Here is a basic set for you to copy. Cut each column into a single "bone" so that you end up with 10 strips.

Index	1	2	3	4	5	6	7	8	9
1	0/1	0/2	0/3	0/4	0/5	0/6	0/7	0/8	0/9
2	0/2	0/4	0/6	0/8	1/0	1/2	1/4	1/6	1/8
3	0/3	0/6	0/9	1/2	1/5	1/8	2/1	2/4	2/7
4	0/4	0/8	1/2	1/6	2/0	2/4	2/8	3/2	3/6
5	0/5	1/0	1/5	2/0	2/5	3/0	3/5	4/0	4/5
6	0/6	1/2	1/8	2/4	3/0	3/6	4/2	4/8	5/4
7	0/7	1/4	2/1	2/8	3/5	4/2	4/9	5/6	6/3
8	0/8	1/6	2/4	3/2	4/0	4/8	5/6	6/4	7/2
9	0/9	1/8	2/7	3/6	4/5	5/4	6/3	7/2	8/1

Napier's bones work by reproducing multiplication tables. In the top rectangle on each bone, you'll see a single digit from 1 to 9. In the 9 rectangles below, you'll find the first 9 multiples of the digit in the top square. Every multiple is divided into two parts by a diagonal: the units written on one side and the tens on the other.

Since each bone contains a multiplication table of a number from 0 to 9, we can use the bones as shortcuts to multiplying large numbers. The trick is in breaking down the multiplicand into units, tens, hundreds and thousands, and then multiplying each by the multiplier.

For example, let's say you want to multiply 6 x 739. This would be the equivalent of multiplying

(6 x 700) + (6 x 30) + (6 x 9)

By placing the 7, 3 and 9 bones next to one another (with the Index bone in front), row 6 gives the answer to the equation (6 x 739) by multiplying the units, tens, hundreds and thousands for you. The diagonals on the bones simply show you which numbers to add to get the final product.

Index	7	3	9
1	0 / 7	0 / 3	0 / 9
2	1 / 4	0 / 6	1 / 8
3	2 / 1	0 / 9	2 / 7
4	2 / 8	1 / 2	3 / 6
5	3 / 5	1 / 5	4 / 5
6	4 / 2	1 / 8	5 / 4
7	4 / 9	2 / 1	6 / 3
8	5 / 6	2 / 4	7 / 2
9	6 / 3	2 / 7	8 / 1

Here is another way to show the same equation:

```
6 x 7        = 4 2      (6 x 700)
6 x   3      =   1 8    (6 x  30)
6 x     9    =     5 4  (6 x   9)
_____
6 x 739      = 4 4 3 4
```

units
tens
hundreds
thousands

Division Dowels

These magical rulers only *look* complicated. They are actually easier to use than Napier's bones. All you need to do is follow the arrows to an answer that is right every time. To prepare for this trick, just copy the set of 11 division dowels on page 37.

1 Ask the audience for a single-digit long-division problem. The dividend can be up to 10 digits long, but cannot have repeat digits. Let's say the audience shouts, "6957 divided by 6!"

2 Select the following cards from your special division deck: 6, 9, 5, 7 (the digits in the dividend), as well as the RD card (for remainders and divisors). Arrange the cards in sequence. A close-up of the top 6 rows is on the right.

3 Since 6 is the divisor, look at row 6. Begin at the topmost number in the far left rectangle of row 6. Then simply follow the lines to the right. You should end up with a quotient of 1159, remainder 3.

Q	6	Q	9	Q	5	Q	7	R	D
3		4		2		3		0	
8		9		7		8		1	2
2		3		1		2		0	
5		6		5		5		1	3
8		9		8		9		2	
1		2		1		1		0	
4		4		3		4		1	4
6		7		6		6		2	
9		9		8		9		3	
1		1		1		1		0	
3		3		3		3		1	
5		5		5		5		2	5
7		7		7		7		3	
9		9		9		9		4	
1		1		0		1		0	
2		3		2		2		1	
4		4		4		4		2	6
6		6		5		6		3	
7		8		7		7		4	
9		9		9		9		5	

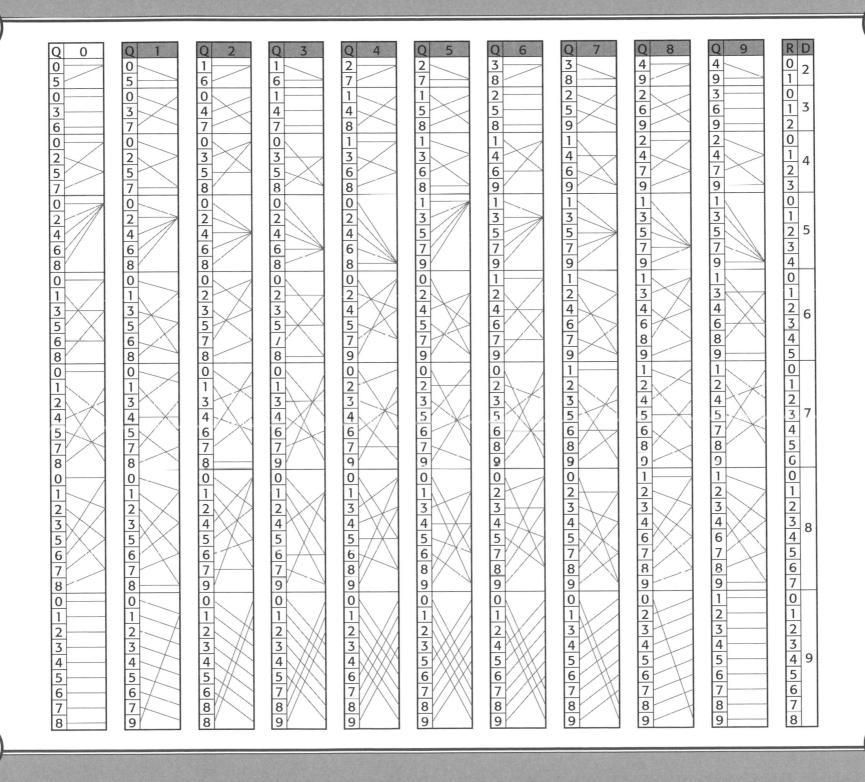

How does this trick work?

No arithmetic operation is as dreaded as long division. To calculate an answer, you need to compare, divide, multiply, subtract and "bring down the number" while keeping track of place-value spaces. Each individual step is easy, but you have to do them in a special order. There are a lot of places where errors can occur as you work through the problem!

Thankfully, *you* have a set of magical division dowels. These rulers were developed by Frenchmen Henri Genaille and Edouard Lucas in the 1800s. Genaille and Lucas were patient enough to work out all the possible quotients and values that one needs to "bring down" in a long-division sequence. They recorded the possibilities in a table and then added lines of direction to help the user perform the calculation accurately and efficiently.

For example, if you were asked to divide 759 by 6 using the steps in traditional long division, you would begin by asking yourself, "How many times does 6 go into 7?" The answer is 1.

Notice that this is the first number circled on the dividing dowels.

When you subtract 6 from 7, you get 1. Notice that on the dowels, the line directs you to 1 position below the first.

If you were to do the traditional steps, multiplying, subtracting and bringing down, you would be taking away 12 from 15: a difference of 3. Notice that the arrow drops 3 positions.

Again, performing the traditional sequence of multiplying, subtracting and bringing down would result in subtracting 36 from 39: a difference of 3, which in this case is the remainder located on the R rod. So 759 ÷ 6 = 126 R3.

Copy and cut out the strips on the previous page and try some long division — just for the *fun* of it!

Take a Bow

Someday, you may see a magician toss a ball high into the air once, twice, three times, and then — *hocus-pocus!* — make it vanish. You may wonder how she did the trick. But unlike those baffled audience members scratching their heads all around you, you'll know that she has no supernatural powers.

Like all great conjurers, she has simply learned and perfected a few little-known techniques.

After reading and practicing the tricks in this book, you'll know that mathemagicians don't have supernatural powers either. But they can still surprise an audience with special tricks of the mathematics trade.

With practice, you will be able to perform feats of mind even more breathtaking than a vanishing ball.

Mathemagic is real, and there are many more tricks waiting to be known (or perhaps even discovered) by you. Even though this book has ended, your apprenticeship has just begun. *Mathakazam!*

Glossary

Addition: the process of joining two or more numbers together to produce one number, which is known as the sum

Binary Number System: a number system that represents numeric values using only two digits: 0 and 1

Calculating: the process of performing the mathematical computing operations (addition, subtraction, multiplication and division)

Complementary Number: two numbers that sum to a power of 10. For example, 3 and 7 are complementary because they add up to 10. Also 22 and 78 are complementary because they add up to 100, and 466 and 534 are complementary because they sum to 1000 and so on.

Composite Number: a number with more than 2 factors

Decimal System: a system for writing any number using only ten symbols: 0, 1, 2, 3, 4, 5, 6, 7, 8 and 9. Also called the base ten system.

Diagonal: the straight line that joins any two non-adjacent vertices of a polygon

Diagram: a figure that represents mathematical information visually

Digits: a term to describe the ten symbols in the Arabic number system: 0, 1, 2, 3, 4, 5, 6, 7, 8, 9

Dividend: the number that is to be divided by a specific number (the divisor)

Divisible: a number that can be evenly divided by another number without a remainder

Division: the inverse operation of multiplication. The process of determining how many groups of one number are contained within another number.

Divisor: the number that will divide the dividend exactly

Equation: a mathematical statement that communicates two equal expressions (usually written horizontally; separated into left and right sides; and containing an equal [=] sign)

Equivalent: having the same value or amount. For example, 3 one-thirds are equal to one whole, and 2 one-quarters are equal to one half.

Expanded Notation: a system of writing numbers to show respective place value positions

Face: any flat surface on a three-dimensional shape

Factor: one of two or more numbers that when multiplied together produce a third number (the product). A number that divides exactly into another number.

Horizontal Line: a line that lies flat at 0° and is parallel to the horizon

Multiple: the number (or product) that results when two numbers are multiplied

Multiplicand: the number that is being multiplied by the multiplier

Multiplier: the number of times that you are adding the multiplicand to itself

Place Value: the value of a digit determined by its position in a number

Prediction: an estimate or guess

Prime Factor: a factor that is also a prime number

Prime Number: any number that is divisible only by 1 and itself

Product: the result when two numbers are multiplied

Quotient: the number obtained by dividing one number by another

Rectangle: a quadrilateral (parallelogram) with four right angles and two pairs of opposite equivalent parallel sides

Remainder: the portion of the dividend that remains when two numbers are divided

Running Total: a total that is continually changing to account for added items

Subtract: to take one number away from another number

Sum: the combined total of two or more numbers through the process of addition

Vertical: a line that is upright and at a right angle to the horizon